How To Find All Missing Persons / Unsolved Cases. And Collect All Reward Offers. Volume XXXXII. THE CASE OF CALEB ALYN BROWN

DAVID GOMADZA

www.twofuture.world

How To Find All Missing Persons / Unsolved Cases. And
Collect All Reward Offers. THE CASE OF CALEB ALYN BROWN

Copyright © 2024 David Gomadza

All rights reserved.

Paperback ISBN: 9798328887090

How To Find All Missing Persons / Unsolved Cases. And Collect All Reward Offers. THE CASE OF CALEB ALYN BROWN

DEDICATION

To a better future.

How To Find All Missing Persons / Unsolved Cases. And
Collect All Reward Offers. THE CASE OF CALEB ALYN BROWN

How To Find All Missing Persons / Unsolved Cases. And
Collect All Reward Offers. THE CASE OF CALEB ALYN BROWN

CONTENTS

How To Find All Missing Persons /
Unsolved Cases.
And Collect All Reward Offers. Volume XXXXII
THE CASE OF CALEB ALN BROWN 1
Afterlife Conversation.

and The Court Of Creation.   5

The Killers.   20

How To Find All Missing Persons / Unsolved Cases. And
Collect All Reward Offers. THE CASE OF CALEB ALYN BROWN

How To Find All Missing Persons / Unsolved Cases. And
Collect All Reward Offers. THE CASE OF CALEB ALYN BROWN

ACKNOWLEDGMENTS

Tomorrow's World Order

How To Find All Missing Persons / Unsolved Cases. And
Collect All Reward Offers. THE CASE OF CALEB ALYN BROWN

How To Find All Missing Persons / Unsolved Cases. And Collect All Reward Offers. Volume XXXXII. THE CASE OF CALEB ALN BROWN

BACKGROUND INFORMATION

Since early December the Scotland County Sheriff's Office has been investigating the disappearance of 20-year-old Caleb Alyn "Draco" Brown. Brown was last seen on Reach Orchard Road in Wagram on Dec. 1 around 7:36 p.m.

He was last seen wearing a grey Nike zip-up jacket, a black shirt, black jeans and multicolored Puma shoes.

He's 5'5, 150 lbs with orange and brown dreadlocks and green eyes.

If you have any information regarding the whereabouts of Caleb Alyn Brown please contact the Scotland County Sheriff's Office at 910-266-4332 Ext. 5. or you can anonymously give a tip to the Scotland County Crime Stoppers at 910-266-8146.

Reach Katelin Gandee at kgandee@laurinburgexchange.com.

How To Find All Missing Persons / Unsolved Cases. And
Collect All Reward Offers. THE CASE OF CALEB ALYN BROWN

TOMORROW'S WORLD ORDER'S PERSPECTIVES

USE OF PREDEFINED AFTERLIFE PARAMETERS

These guide souls the moment it exist the human body on its journey to Yahweh the creator these define what to do and what to expect as you go to hell or heaven if a souk leaves earth it enters ozone orbit and instantly everything reboots for it to start a new phase of life after living the earth's body now what happens is that it enters the ozone orbit and a simply click caused by the sudden drop of pressure from -1186 to – 20 means the bottom shaft of the soul will lift rapidly and this pushes its back into the air higher than its head best example is a penguin but with real human legs and head just the shape now God created a life predefined program for them instead of asking what should I do and where should I go they instantly know from predefined stencils if you did well and talked most about God then heaven is for you if you did evil and talked more about the devil then the devil is yours now if we Ask what can be of humans without souks this is the answer dead forever your soul is you a new transformation to the electromagnetic waves life where you see Yahweh for the first time and praise him and wish you had seen him a long time ago because of his Majesty and will always be there forever now what are all these you may ask these are rules to be guided by in the creation court in short it has everything humans know about the judges and the presiding judge who will always be Yahweh and 84 angels surrounding the altar 28 high priests who always say Yahweh have mercy on humans and 74 smaller courts priests who always say Yahweh has mercy on humans and 96 princesses who say glory to Yahweh forever and ever amen we have 96 elders who always say if I can why he can't meaning if the devil can drink blood why can't Yahweh who created the devil and blood do the same now this is not the same as saying if the devil can kill why can Yahweh its more on professional grounds rather than challenging now if we look at the inside of the court we have 81 priests surrounding the altar who say Yahweh be merciful to humans but if they disobey you we put hem on trial for you and kill them for

you almighty Yahweh inside this is a round circle where Yahweh sits and asks questions now if we look deep inside the court you will see that there are other things that resemble earth high courts like benches and chairs 10 times human sizes for the gods who are so enormous 2 are equal to 84 billion humans in size
predefined parameters for humans after death as in know what is inside is a large size of books the book of creation is among them with 10897867892836789012348678901245861789011 pages and is divided into humans first then chapter for animals then a chapter for angles then a chapter for gods and a chapter for Joseph Yahweh's best friend and a chapter for Yahweh's best friend's wife Anna and a chapter for Yahweh's wife Catitighit and lastly a chapter for Yahweh and recently a chapter for davidgomadza as Yahweh's representative on earth marking the new beginnings starting in 2025

1. tell us who killed you
2. tell us what killed you
3. tell us why and who killed you
4. tell us why you died
5. tell us what could have been done and is not done
6. tell us what could be and why
7. tell is when this happened
8. tell us why this is so
9. tell us why this is so
10. what can be done to improve this

What does the book of creation say about davidgomadza David Gomadza is the first and last ruler to be appointed by Yahweh fir the next 25 billion years and will act as his representative on earth deciding cases and upholding his principles on earth and as such has been entitled to 489 trillion dollars in assets this number signifies eternity among humans and the beginning of a new Era chapter 7867892802893862841890287689018320867890123486789018236487289128610 Creation manual the new Era of new electromagnetic wave conduit signed and dated by Yahweh himself on 27may2024 at 237800 Yatime
creation.universe.ya.start.end.find.davidgomadza.ya.askya.ya

Ask.read.creation.manucreation.universe.ya.start.end.find.davidgoma
askya.ya

Ask.rulesofthecourt.start.now.start
David Gomadza welcome the rules of court are guiding principles that tell you what to do and how to do it first you must always say I believe in the court of creation and I shall abide by he rules of this court and shall always do things according to the rules of this court in deciding the cases I am assigned to you must ask what can be done so that you know all your options before making choices the court system will make it easy to check files and ask the outcomes of the decision ask the court the final decision in any case.

THE AFTERLIFE CONVERSATION AND THE COUNCIL OF CREATION'S ANAYLSIS.

>   deposit a quarter today the rest tomorrow i tell you exactly what happened..
>
>   after i finish then tell the police
>   deposit here today this is what happened i work for Yahweh and tomorrow's world order www.twofuture.world
>   00447719210295
>   deposit a quarter today so i finish
>   https://twofuture.world/donate
>
>   caleb alyn brown
>   coordinates heaven
>   78.987654238
>   62.78969084
>   you died a horrific death something ate half side of you and you then died of
>   1. a loss of blood
>   2. lack of breathe as all air went out
>   3. dehydration as all water ran out
>   4. suffocation as all oxygen escaped
>   were you teared into two yes by asepen arotuv he said give me

the money or i tear you like a dog into two with my own hands and i said okay but did not give him the money then he said if i can then i can but you cheating because you have money i swear if you give me i let you go because i am in no mood to argue with you i can do this all day but time is not on my side so what is it going to be money or be torn into two so i laughed because he appeared to cry everytime he spoke and that sounded unreal then i said bitch if i was in your position i would say before i finish talking he grab me by my belt trousers and ravaged me in and out of unconscious by the way he shock me and the next thing i know is that i was literally naked down to the boxer when he said hold the other side and instantly two very big guys appeared from no way and said hold him then he pulled my other leg but i did not think this was possible but it took less than 2 minutes and i was open literally open i swear and i ran out of breath inside for the first time i heard things talking one said how can we save him without air what happened to him he is not breathing or air is liking out then another alarm that said how can he breath without air where is all the air if i knew he is this dumb i would have escaped then that means we are all going to die then another that said quick oxygen is running out if you can please refill yours fir him and whatever this things was refilled instantly and said i run out me too i have to leave or in heaven they will ask what happened who you didn't leave when you know he will die the problem is that they opened him from the groin to the neck so there is nothing on earth we can do we can only look and hope that something good come out of this but as it stands he is breathing his last nothing because oxygen is literally zero i never seen what he is going through as an angel of Yahweh instantly he cried last cry before death that removes air so that the suction effect withdraws the soul out of the compartment then it did as the soul escapes but stood in front of him for the first time and cried hard then left going to Yahweh but it fell and died there and there but i saw this and quickly took it and ran to Yahweh with it who said why risk your own life flying at speeds like that for a human a crook for that matter and i said that is your job to decide i calculated the risk it was okay

coordinates where body is
82.78906834890
88.789824567890
https://www.facebook.com/share/p/jmejixz5hssxln6p/

i am caleb alyn brown i am just 21 years old i was born on 21 march and every year i go out with my crew to a pub called ayertert meaning hot air vibes that i love i am into hip-hop and reggae and this night i met a lot of people congratulating me then i met rass who said if i can the. and left then returned and said but then left then came back and said if you can then what but kept silent then said what i have is not from this planet i have the power of the gods jupiter in particular and said if i can then i can show you one day then he said okay i will then he left but returned later with two very big guys and said i can but if you can't then what then left i liked the way he talked he never finish his sentences so i always try to guess what he is talking about then he said i can if you can but then stopped and said if i can then what can be but trouble then left later he just said buy if you like the way i talk then stopped and i looked confused and i said what's to buy then he said time moved from one time zone to the other but we can be on the same side but then again you like Yahweh then stopped i know people confuse rasta with god so i said i like Jah not Ya then he looked surprised and said okay but who is better and powerful mine is Yahweh and you go with Jah for 5 000 i will win the bet so be prepared to play the game so i thought it's what boys do in situations like this so i said you can't do that can we instead play for money and he said okay but you pay tonight or die i said you die bitch with that girl lying voice you go down but he said i am the man that can be i can tear you into two literally in less than 2 seconds and i refused that and said it takes a crane to apart me so we battled it out i won money but i realised that he let me win the money then tear me into two but that had not sunk i said if that was real i could have heard that before but he said it's new fashion i will let you wear that for a while but i need the final bet give me 800 dollars first i had won 300 from him so i said let's battle fair choose something to do then we free style until one wins then he said i can't i need the money so that i can go then he said if you don't then your life is ending and mine just beginning and he cried honestly and i said i said it can't be that bad don't be a bitch let's freestyle until one wins then he said i have medical condition i need the money more than you so give it to me nicely i respect you but what can i do so i gave him back his 300nand said okay then i can only give you 200 now i am in your position i have 300 and a nerdcall condition so I laughed at my wits and said i can if you can then he said okay so you want to split me look at me plus you are just jelly real man should have understood and say i know take the money that means you are more valuable but you choose death over 500 dollars that is what your live is worthy and it started to sink that he was testing my wits but i did it because it felt like he admired me so not to humiliate him i took the challenge because in the end i was going to give him the money but i wanted him to work for the money then he said i admit you are a gentlemen and can tear like tissue in the toilet that hurts that i nearly punched him then he said you hurting bro truth hurts and i said okay take the money i will go back all alone we were walking betting and i don't even know where we were going then he said hold him then two big men hold one side of me the leg and chest and heard and in a flash he pulled my leg so hard that all my clothes literally tore in half then he said now give me the money and see what happens too i only smiled and died i heard long ago 2 seconds shutting down counting and flew up the skies until a voice said you have arrived at the reception and an angel pretty but with nothing at all at the bottom said you will be seen soon and left and ever since i was there until when someone said if you like we can interview you then fix if possible what needs fixing.

caleb alyn brown
vitals and statistics at time of death
heart 78
rtc 20
rtl 30

rtd 29
rtk 39
rt0 26
rt1 27
rt2 28
rt3 20
rt8 29
rt9 30
rt7 21
rt6 8
rt4 9
rt2 6
rt8 10
rt21 7
rt22 8
rt3 9
rt4 6
rt5 8
rt6 9
rt7 8
rt8 9
rt9 0
rtt 21
rt3 02
rt9 07
rts2 is 7
rt9 is now n0 which read now as rt

i care less about humans who got about challenging others when they have nothing to show for it you died for a reason all you had to say was that rass you the start state of California prison but to be released this year in June or July and promised to take out another weak brown for treated bad in prison but only brown made him feel like a real powerful God Jupiter who tear people for a living his coordinates are 82.19787898 87.678987.678st california prison usa

i said I can tear a human being into two but no one believed me now you two aropt astert real name toperer otwtota and atoder aster who acted as his henchmen were there and carried him covered in so much blood that they emptied his body and said to the gods let them drink the blood I took 800 only but it's better because someone died for it if someone asks then he died for 500 because 300 was mine and they laughed hard until a pity at coordinates
82.3687890284
83.298783.29870
South east of a place called once I was a goat then became a bull now I just eat both now laugh in local language
Ask for satop around that area because they kept saying do you know satop he live around here but if you don't know this guy then you don't know anyone and you will never be discovered and die here
I am satop I find all lost and find here but at a huge price for example Caleb Alyn brown father was asked on TV if he is willing to die for his son or let his son die for his sins he said I can die for his sins but who will dare touch my boy and never be afraid again
They then threw him in a pit and covered it with hood and threw everything as well and said if God is there then we have everything to be afraid if not forever no one will guess and we will never remove everything we let the killer guide the place forever but someone removed the killer the next day of burial he said I can't kill a useless one and guide him for eternity anyone need real help
Jupiter can tear your enemy into two and left but he was there today but to scare Caleb off after we amended him

...I found God...visit www.twofuture.world

How To Find All Missing Persons / Unsolved Cases. And Collect All Reward Offers. THE CASE OF CALEB ALYN BROWN

THE CLAIM

the reward offer

THE COLLECTION

www.twofuture.world/donate

ABOUT DAVID GOMADZA

visit www.twofuture.world

signed david gomadza
ask.davidgomadzaauthorised.licensed.checkya.askya.ya

19 June 2024 12.0 pm
scotland
00447719210295
davidgomadza@hotmail.com
info@twofuture.world

Visit www.twofuture.world

The practical guide on how to solve the missing persons or unsolved cases with reward value of $1 million each. Methodology: all the tools you need.

THE PRACTICAL GUIDE ON

HOW TO SOLVE THE MISSING PERSONS OR UNSOLVED CASES

WITH REWARD VALUE OF $1 Million Each.
METHODOLOGY: ALL THE TOOLS YOU NEED.

David Gomadza
www.twofuture.world

www.ingramcontent.com/pod-product-compliance
Lightning Source LLC
Chambersburg PA
CBHW031524210526
45464CB00007B/3016